Martha Berry

Martha Berry

By Mary Kay Phelan
Illustrated by Charles W. Walker

Thomas Y. Crowell Company   New York

CROWELL BIOGRAPHIES
Edited by Susan Bartlett Weber

JANE ADDAMS *by Gail Faithfull Keller*
LEONARD BERNSTEIN *by Molly Cone*
MARTHA BERRY *by Mary Kay Phelan*
WILT CHAMBERLAIN *by Kenneth Rudeen*
CESAR CHAVEZ *by Ruth Franchere*
SAMUEL CLEMENS *by Charles Michael Daugherty*
CHARLES DREW *by Roland Bertol*
THE MAYO BROTHERS *by Jane Goodsell*
GORDON PARKS *by Midge Turk*
THE RINGLING BROTHERS *by Molly Cone*
JACKIE ROBINSON *by Kenneth Rudeen*
ELEANOR ROOSEVELT *by Jane Goodsell*
MARIA TALLCHIEF *by Tobi Tobias*
JIM THORPE *by Thomas Fall*
MALCOLM X *by Arnold Adoff*

Copyright © 1972 by Mary Kay Phelan

Illustrations copyright © 1972 by Charles W. Walker

All rights reserved. Except for use in a review, the reproduction or utilization of this work in any form or by any electronic, mechanical, or other means, now known or hereafter invented, including xerography, photocopying, and recording, and in any information storage and retrieval system is forbidden without the written permission of the publisher. Published simultaneously in Canada by Fitzhenry & Whiteside Limited, Toronto.

Manufactured in the United States of America

L.C. Card 77-158699
ISBN 0-690-52112-X
(Library Edition 0-690-52113-8)

1 2 3 4 5 6 7 8 9 10

Martha Berry

A CROWELL BIOGRAPHY

Three little barefoot boys on tiptoe peered through the cabin window. Inside they saw a pretty lady reading a book.

Martha Berry had a feeling someone was watching her. She looked up just in time to see three pairs of bright eyes disappear. She moved quickly to the doorway.

There beside the cabin stood the boys in their dusty shirts and patched overalls. On their heads were the ragged straw hats that all the mountain children wore.

Martha smiled. "Please come in," she said. "I would like to talk to you."

At first the boys were shy. Martha gave them some cookies. Then she asked if they went to school. The boys shook their heads. School, they said, was miles and miles and miles away.

"Would you like to hear some Bible stories?" the young woman asked. The boys nodded. There was a Bible at home, they said, but no one could read it.

The boys plopped down on the floor to listen. As Martha told story after story, the people in the Bible seemed to come alive. The boys' eyes grew wider and wider. They forgot about the time. When the sun began to go down, Martha said they had better go home now. But she invited them to come back the next Sunday.

Watching the small boys leave for home, Martha felt sad. She knew what kind of homes the children lived in. They were one-room log cabins with dirt floors. Often there was not a single window.

All the cooking was done over an open fireplace. But there was never enough to eat. Greasy

pork and ground corn day after day made the children thin and pale. They were often sick, but no doctor was called. There was no money to pay him.

Martha began thinking of her own childhood. She had lived all her life in a large white house called Oak Hill. She had known so much happiness. These children had known so little.

Thomas Berry, Martha's father, had settled

near Rome, Georgia, many years ago. Part of the countryside around Rome is flat, fertile land. The other part rises toward thickly wooded mountains. These are the Appalachian Mountains. They stretch almost a thousand miles from the North through the South.

Mr. Berry bought some of the flat land and began growing cotton. Then he met Frances Rhea, the girl who was to become Martha's mother. They were married and went to Oak Hill to live.

During the years he was a bachelor, Mr. Berry had made many friends among the men who lived back in the mountains. When the Civil War began, he formed his own infantry company with these men. Side by side they fought through the terrible war. After that he was always called "Captain."

When the war was over, Captain Berry returned to Oak Hill. His cotton crops were ruined. But Frances managed to save their home. Together they began to rebuild what they had lost.

The next year, on October 7, 1866, Martha was born. She was the second of eight children. With two brothers and five sisters, she always had plenty of playmates. In summer the children went horseback riding and took fishing trips. In the winter they made sleds from barrel staves and

scattered pine needles on the hills to make the sleds go faster.

There were only a few schools in Georgia in the 1870's. The Berry children were taught by Miss Ida McCullough, who came to the house every day. After lessons were finished, Miss McCullough took them on long walks. She taught them to love the out-of-doors. With her they often hunted flowers in the woods—the lady's-slippers and Indian pipes. They looked at the leaves and stems through a magnifying glass.

Martha told her father she could learn her lessons much better if she could study out of doors in a log cabin. So Captain Berry built a one-room cabin for his children. It was in a grove of trees near Oak Hill.

The times Martha liked to remember most were the horseback rides with her father. Sometimes he took her along when he rode up into the mountains to visit the men who had fought with him in the Civil War. He told her a great deal about these mountain people.

Their grandfathers and great-grandfathers had come to Georgia from England and Scotland, he said. They were strong men and women, and

very intelligent. They settled in the Appalachian Mountains, hoping to farm. They built their log cabins and cleared away the tangled weeds so they could plant cotton and corn. The soil had much red clay. Often some crops failed. Rakes and plows rusted. Year after year there was less and less to eat. But the families stayed on. They had no money to move farther west where land was better for farming.

Captain Berry was a generous man. He wanted to help the people. But he explained to Martha that it was important to know how to give.

"If you *hand* things to needy people," he said, "you take away their pride. *Lend* them seed and tools to grow their own crops. Then you will have given wisely." Very often Martha and her father went visiting with sacks of seed tucked in the saddlebag.

When she was seventeen years old, Martha was sent to a boarding school in Baltimore, Maryland. She stayed only one year because she was unhappy there. She longed to be back with her family.

After she returned, everyone noticed how pretty she was. She had gray-blue eyes, a fair skin, and curly black hair. She was lively and full of fun. Many young men invited her to parties. There was one she liked better than all the others.

Then her father became very ill. He told Martha that he wanted to leave her some money and

some land across the road from Oak Hill. After he died, Martha was very lonely.

Mrs. Berry had to manage the plantation alone. She worked late at night on the account books and was up early in the morning to direct the cotton pickers. Martha had to help care for the smaller children. When the young man she liked asked her to set a wedding date, she said they would have to wait awhile.

Several years passed. The little cabin where the Berry children had gone to school was no longer needed for lessons. Martha decided to make it her own special hideaway. Here she went to read and relax and dream. Many times she thought about her father and how good he had been to the mountain people. How could she help them? What was the best way to "give wisely," as her father had put it?

Martha was reading in this cabin when the three little boys peeked through the window. The boys returned the next Sunday to listen to more stories. Martha hurried out to greet them and the sisters who had tagged along. First they would play a game, Martha suggested.

She brought out a magnifying glass and showed

the children how their hands looked under the glass. Then she brought pails of water and plenty of soap. After they had scrubbed hard, the chil-

dren looked through the glass again. Their hands were so clean! It was hard to believe. "There is no perfume quite like soap and water," Martha said. After the game was finished, she told some Bible stories. The children begged for more.

Sunday after Sunday the boys and girls came to the cabin. They brought others. Before any stories were told, they always played the "soap-and-water game." Soon fathers and mothers, grandfathers and grandmothers, came with the children. The Sunday crowds began to overflow the little log cabin.

Martha decided she must start other Sunday schools. She remembered some old wooden buildings back in the mountains. They had once been used as churches. So she hitched her pony to a buggy and drove along the rocky mountain roads to find places for her Sunday schools.

The buildings were in worse condition than she had expected. Windows were broken. The roofs were full of holes. Still they were places where people could meet. They would have to do. Before long she started three different Sunday schools. Each Sunday she rode from one to another to tell the Bible stories. The people started to call her "the Sunday Lady," a name which made her very proud.

Martha began to feel that she was not doing enough. The eager children asked many questions. How could they learn to read? How could they write their names? How could they work numbers?

Martha knew that one way to help the mountain people was by teaching their children to help themselves. Could she do it? Martha didn't know. She only knew she had to try. So she made plans to start a weekday school.

On the land her father had given her, she decided to build a one-room schoolhouse. She bought some lumber and hired a carpenter. Then she asked several of the bigger boys to help. From boards and boxes Martha made benches for the children to sit on. Her desk was a big wooden packing case. Outside she planted bright flowers and shrubs.

At first Martha found the teaching very hard. She knew so little about how to do it. Her family said she was wasting her time. Her younger sister Frances came to help with the classes. Sometimes the older boys were restless. They laughed at the students who wanted to study. They played tricks on the teacher. But they soon learned Martha had a temper. She caught them by the ears and led them out of class.

In spite of the troubles the first few months, the boys and girls were learning to read and write. More students came. Martha added two rooms to the little building. Then she decided to start more schools in the old wooden church buildings she used on Sundays. She asked some friends to help with the teaching.

Another year passed and another. The man to whom Martha was engaged kept asking when they could be married. She didn't want to stop teaching. She kept saying, "Later, later." Finally Martha broke her engagement. She loved the man, but she loved her mountain children even more. She couldn't have both. She knew she could never give up her work with the boys and girls.

Most of the children learned quickly. Still Martha was not content. Vacations were too long. When school started again, the pupils had for-

gotten too much of what they had learned. Some of the children had to walk a long distance. In bad weather they stayed away. Worst of all, the boys often had to miss school to help with the farm work at home.

Martha began dreaming of a new kind of school for the mountain boys. It would be a school where they could live, month after month. They would not only learn how to read and write. They would plant crops. They would take care of the livestock. Each boy would work as well as study.

By doing the work themselves, the boys would also learn better ways to farm. No one had ever heard of such an idea before, but Martha wanted to try it. The day-schools would continue, she said, but she wanted a boarding school for boys, too. It would be called the Boys' Industrial School.

Martha's family was very upset. Her mother said she was already working too hard. Her sisters asked her if she didn't ever want to get married. Martha paid no attention. She was determined that this dream should come true.

An architect was asked to draw plans for a little two-story dormitory. Martha said the outside gate would be called "the gate of opportunity." It must open two ways, "for those coming in to learn and those going out to give the world what they have learned."

The new building took almost all the money

Martha's father had left her. The day it was finished, she ran to the new school bell and began tugging on the rope. She rang it and rang it and rang it. Everyone came running and asked what was the matter. Martha laughed. "It means the beginning of a new day," she said.

There was no money for furnishing the new dormitory. Martha took a sofa and a bed from her own room at Oak Hill. She asked friends to give her any furniture and dishes they wanted to get rid of. Beds, desks, and bookcases were built from old packing cases.

Finally everything was ready. Martha hired two teachers and moved into the dormitory her-

self. She was going to teach and help with the cooking, too. She also bought a cow to supply milk. The new school opened on January 13, 1902.

On the first day five boys arrived. They had few clothes and little money. But Martha said the boys could work to pay for their schooling. They chopped wood, cleared away the underbrush, and helped in the kitchen.

Word about the new school spread through the mountain country. One student brought a team of oxen to help pay his tuition. Another arrived with a few chickens. It was not much, they said, but maybe it would help.

Before and after classes the boys planted vegetable gardens so there would be food to eat. They set out fruit trees and took turns milking the cow. After lessons were finished in the evenings, Martha played games and told stories to the boys.

It took a lot of money to keep the school going. And Martha had so little left. She was always worried about where she would get more. One evening she heard one of the boys saying a prayer. He told the Lord he had read in the paper about people in New York who gave money to schools. Then he asked the Lord to give Miss Berry strength to go up North and tell people how much they needed things.

Martha thought about the boy's prayer. She was frightened about going so far away. "But," she said later, "when somebody prays for you, you just have to do something."

After she arrived in New York, Martha called some friends she had known in the Baltimore school. They discouraged her. Then one friend remembered a minister who might be interested. She went to his church and talked to a group of people. They gave her some money. They also gave her names of other people who might help. Before Martha left New York she had five hundred dollars. It was the first of many trips she made all over the United States to get money for her school.

As the years went by, new boys kept coming. More buildings were put up. More teachers joined the staff. By this time the state of Georgia had started more schools for younger children in the region. Martha's classes in the old wooden church buildings were no longer needed. She now spent all her time at the Boys' Industrial School.

By 1907 the story of Martha's work with the mountain children was well known. A friend told President Theodore Roosevelt about the school. He asked Martha to come and see him.

She was very pleased about the invitation. But she was also a little frightened about meeting someone as important as a president of the United States. When she arrived at the White House, Martha showed President Roosevelt photographs of the cabins that her students came from. Some

of the cabin walls, she said, had "holes large enough for a dog to leap through."

Then she showed pictures of the boys in their school uniforms—blue work shirts and overalls. Some were studying in the classrooms. Others were harvesting corn and picking tomatoes. Still others were milking cows in the barn.

President Roosevelt smiled. "Young woman," he said, "most people are dreamers with visions on paper. You're making it go! Let me help you give the same chance to the girls down in Georgia."

A school for girls was something Martha had dreamed about for a long time. Ever since the boys' school opened, girls had wanted to come, too. Many people said that Martha already had too much to do, but she decided to start a girls' school anyway.

She knew just the place. It was a gently rising hill about a mile from the boys' school. The boys helped cut down trees and saw them into logs. They also helped build the dormitory and schoolhouse for the girls.

On Thanksgiving Day, 1909, the girls' school was opened. Like the boys, the girls had to work as well as study. They planted their own vegetable gardens. They were taught to cook meals that were healthful but didn't cost much money.

They learned how to spin thread and weave cloth.

Soon after President Roosevelt's term in office ended, he came to visit The Berry School. The students greeted him with loud cheers. Martha showed him the classrooms and dormitories built among the tall pine trees. He inspected the peach orchards and the rows of grapevines planted along the mountainside. He watched the girls can peas, beans, and tomatoes that they had raised in their gardens. He saw the boys plowing the fields and talked to them about their crops.

Later in the day President Roosevelt made a speech. He said he hoped each student would be "a lifter and not a leaner." He was glad the students were learning to be leaders in whatever they chose to do.

The students liked what President Roosevelt had said. The next morning they adopted his words

for the school slogan: "Be a lifter, not a leaner."

In 1917 America entered World War I, and many boys joined the army. Teachers left for officers' training camps. There was so much work and so few hands to do it. Some said Martha should close her schools, but her answer was a firm "No, indeed." The war ended in November 1918. Students and teachers returned. Soon everything was running smoothly again.

At Oak Hill, Martha's old home, there had been many changes. All the children, except Martha, had married and moved away. Mrs. Berry was alone, though she still directed the work on the plantation. She worried about how hard Martha worked. Yet she was proud of what her daughter was doing.

The boys and girls wanted Miss Berry to know how much they appreciated their fine education.

The boys, with the help of a teacher, built a small cottage on top of Lavendar Mountain. The girls wove the curtains and rugs. They planted a garden with Martha's favorite flowers, and she named the cottage the "House O' Dreams." Martha said it was one of the nicest presents she had ever had.

Whenever there seemed to be too many problems, she climbed the mountain to her cottage. Here she could rest. She liked to remember the little log cabin at Oak Hill where she first dreamed of the school she would build.

Many important people were interested in The Berry Schools. In 1923 the famous automobile maker Henry Ford and his wife came to visit. Mr. Ford believed that people should work with

their hands as well as their heads. He liked what he saw at Martha's schools. The Fords came back year after year to visit. They gave money for many new buildings.

Still Martha was not satisfied. Many of the students who finished the high school courses wanted to stay on and learn more. In the fall of 1926 Martha opened a junior college for these boys and girls. A little while later it became a four-year college.

Martha no longer had to worry about having to close her schools. There was enough money now to keep them going. She received many honors and awards for what she was doing. People all over the world borrowed her idea of schools where students both studied and worked.

As the years passed, Martha's health began to fail. In one of her last speeches she said, "It is wonderful to be allowed to work. It is one of God's greatest gifts. It is a privilege to work for boys and girls you believe in." When she died in 1942, thousands of students and friends were saddened.

Since that time there have been many changes. When there was no longer a need for it, Martha's school for girls was closed. The Boys' Industrial School became Berry Academy. It is a four-year high school that prepares boys for college.

The campus of Berry College keeps growing. There are many new buildings of brick and stone, filled with the finest equipment. Some students are from big cities. Others are from small towns and farms. They come from all over the United States as well as from foreign countries. They study for many different kinds of jobs.

Martha Berry had great dreams for the children she loved. She spent fifty years making those dreams come true. Because of what she did, the "gate of opportunity" was opened to thousands

of boys and girls. Berry Academy and Berry College are proud of their past. The fine education they offer today grew from the work Martha began so many years ago.

ABOUT THE AUTHOR

Mary Kay Phelan has a great talent for making people who once lived and performed great deeds live and perform them again for young readers. Mrs. Phelan regards historical research as both a vocation and an avocation. With her husband she is involved in the production of 8-millimeter films that are widely used in schools and libraries. She is the author of *Four Days in Philadelphia—1776,* which tells the story of the adoption of the Declaration of Independence; *Midnight Alarm,* an account of Paul Revere's ride; a biography of Dr. Florence Sabin; and *The Great Chicago Fire—1871.* She has also written three books in the Crowell Holiday series: *Mother's Day, The Fourth of July,* and *Election Day.*

Mrs. Phelan was born in Baldwin City, Kansas; was graduated from DePauw University in Indiana; and received her M.A. from Northwestern University. She lives with her family in Davenport, Iowa.

ABOUT THE ILLUSTRATOR

Charles W. Walker is particularly drawn to MARTHA BERRY because, having six children, he is naturally interested in the education of the young. He feels that the most sensible form of teaching is a combination of classwork and practical on-the-job participation, which Martha Berry advocated.

Born in Hempstead, New York, Mr. Walker was graduated cum laude from the Syracuse University College of Fine Arts with a Bachelor of Fine Arts degree. He also studied at the Art Students' League in New York.

In addition to illustrating books, he enjoys sketching and painting and is an active member of the Society of Illustrators.

Mr. Walker now lives in Roosevelt, New York, with his wife and children.